WORDS FROM A FEARLESS HEART

A collection of wit, wisdom, and whimsy

LAURA INGALLS WILDER

EDITED BY
STEPHEN W. HINES

THOMAS NELSON PUBLISHERS
Nashville • Atlanta • London • Vancouver

Published in Nashville, Tennessee, by Thomas Nelson, Inc., Publishers, and distributed in Canada by Word Communications, Ltd., Richmond, British Columbia, and in the United Kingdom by Word (UK), Ltd., Milton Keynes, England.

ISBN 0-7852-7723-4

Printed in the United States of America

Contents

~

Introduction: Welcome to Laura's World *v*

1 God's World *1*

2 Proper Perspectives *15*

3 Home and Family *29*

4 Work and Play *39*

5 Virtues and Vices *51*

6 Wit *61*

7 Nation and Society *73*

8 Whimsy *85*

9 Gazing Forward . . . Looking Back *93*

10 Wisdom *105*

11 Life and Truth *115*

12 Relationships *127*

For Gwen—my sunlight at dawn
on the western sea

Welcome to Laura's World

*Y*ou would have liked Laura Ingalls Wilder. There were so many different facets to her character and experience that she was like a shining gem of which the admirer never grew tired. I am such an admirer, for there *is* much to admire in this great lady—perhaps one of the greatest our country has ever produced.

Born in a log cabin deep in the Wisconsin woods just two years after the Civil War, Laura came into a world of change. During her lifetime the reaper, the electric light, the telephone, the automobile, and the airplane were invented and developed. The frontier, which had already been discovered, was fully explored and settled.

Yet it was only toward the end of her life that Mrs. Wilder realized she had witnessed practically the entire American pioneer era. As she put it, she represented a "whole period of American history" too precious to be lost. So in her sixties, she began the pioneer series of children's books that was to make her famous and inspire the *Little House on the Prairie* TV series.

This accomplishment alone would have been enough to give her a special place in the hearts of all Americans who understand that you can't appreciate how far you have come, as a nation and as a people, unless you know where you have begun. No, Mrs. Wilder was not a pessimist about America's future. She felt that America and Americans needed only to be reminded of the things that made them great: not automobiles and airplanes, but self-reliance and character. And it is to her rediscovered journalistic writings that this book turns—to inform us of Laura's point of view about the things that really matter.

Although not all of these excerpts of Laura's early writings are serious, almost all make some point, either humorous or otherwise. All of her words contained in this volume come from the time when Laura observed the wide world from her little farm atop a small Ozark ridge. Though the view may have been limited from her hilltop, her heart's vision was not constricted by any narrowness of soul.

Nature taught her to love beauty, her friends taught her to love others, and her family imbued her with values that last.

Finally, as an editor and as a writer it has been my privilege to provide settings in which these aphoristic gems of Mrs. Wilder's may rest. I send this volume out with the hope that the reader will understand Laura's greatness and humility and be enriched by her words.

The diamond still shines in all its facets.

Stephen W. Hines

1
God's World

Why is the world so beautiful if not for us?

~

I have never lost my childhood delight in going after the cows. I still slip from other things for the sake of the walk through the pastures, down along the creek and over the hill to the farthest corner where the cows are usually found. Many a time, instead of me finding the cows, they, on their journey home, unurged, found me and took me home with them.

~

Going after the Cows

~

Laura Ingalls Wilder was an animal lover. There is no doubt about this fact at all. Not only did she feed turtles on her back doorstep—who would have thought turtles had sense enough to know where to beg for a handout?—but she also kept her dogs like they were members of the family. One of them, Ring, actually ate at the table with her and "the Man of the Place." And every goat on the farm (quite a few over the years) had a name.

Thus, it comes as no surprise that one of Laura's fondest memories from childhood was that of going after the cows. And any one of the fortunate few who have ever

had anything to do with the placid cow can empathize with her experience.

Laura wrote that more often than not it was the cows who brought her home rather than she the cows. There were so many interesting things to see and do along the way! Besides, she really didn't herd the cows. She simply showed up, and they knew what was expected of them and headed off for the barn.

Mrs. Wilder wrote of dipping her feet in the creek and playing among the water plants, forgetting the cows completely. She knew she could do that too. That was the great thing about going after cows—the diversions she could get into along the way as she trailed along rather far behind them.

A boy doing the job might not have noticed flowers, but Laura always did—some of them huge sunflowers growing wild in the fields and considered more like noxious weeds to the farm fathers who had to grow the hay to feed those meandering cows. "That ought to be pure prairie grass out there, not sunflowers or worse, Scottish thistles!" they'd say. There was a lot about farming that could drive the sentimental right out of you, but that never happened to Laura.

So, going after the cows wasn't work really; it was an education in appreciating nature, docile creatures, and the value of a little thoughtful idleness to break the hurry of the day. Mrs. Wilder knew the delight of it all, the just plain restfulness of a pleasant daily routine.

"Here, Bossy, don't go that way! You know where the barn is! Take your time or you'll sour the milk!"

෴

We have a whole five acres for our backyard and all outdoors for our conservatory, filled not only with beautiful flowers, but with grand old trees as well, with running water and beautiful birds, with sunshine and fresh air and all wild, free, beautiful things.

෴

I love to listen to the bird songs every day
And hear the free winds whisper in their play,
Among the tall old trees and sweet wild flowers.
I love to watch the little brook
That gushes from its cool and rocky bed
Deep in the earth. The sky is blue o'er head
And sunbeams dance upon its tiny rivulet.

෴

We are the heirs of the ages; but the estate is entailed, as large estates frequently are, so that while we inherit the earth . . . we have only the use of it while we live and must pass it on to those who come after us. We

hold the property in trust and have no right to
injure it or to lessen its value.

❧

If people could only realize how ridiculous they
appear when they call down the wrath of the
Creator and Ruler of the universe just because they
have jammed their thumbs, I feel sure they would
never be guilty of swearing again. If we call upon
the Mightiest for trivial things, upon whom or what
shall we call in the great moments of life?

❧

Saw mills are now busily at work in the South, and
the timber is fast disappearing before them. . . .
Then only the forests of the Pacific coast will
remain, and they will not last long. Those of us who
have permitted this destruction [of forests] . . . will
wish to hide our faces from the generations we have
robbed.

❧

The voices of nature do not speak so plainly to us as
we grow older.

Now it isn't enough in any garden to cut down the weeds. The cutting out of weeds is important, but cultivating the garden plants is just as necessary. If we want vegetables, we must make them grow, not leave the ground barren where we have destroyed the weeds.

≈

From the still growth of a wild flower to the rush of a mountain torrent . . . every sound in nature has the beauties of harmony.

≈

We cannot go on forever using gasoline in ever increasing quantities without coming at last to the end of the supply.

≈

I love the timid things
That gather round the little watercourse
To listen to the frogs with voices hoarse,
And see the squirrels leap and bound at play.

≈

The Man of the Place worried about the weather. There were dry years in the Dakotas when we were beginning our life together. I said at that time that thereafter I would sow the seed, but the Lord would give the increase, if there was any; for I could not do my work and that of Providence also.

~

The Ingallses' Faith

~

*M*any people naturally wonder about the Ingalls family and the part that religious faith played in their lives. Those who have seen some of the more touching episodes of Michael Landon's *Little House on the Prairie* TV series get a sense—a fairly accurate sense—that the Ingallses were a Christian family.

Ma Ingalls in particular was deeply religious and saw to the Christian education of the girls. When the family finally settled near Walnut Grove, Minnesota, after previous stops in Wisconsin, Kansas, Missouri, and Iowa, they were eager to have a church affiliation. The local Congregational organization welcomed them into fellowship through the rite of baptism, and they became founding members of the First Congregational Church.

This would have occurred in the mid-1870s, and the fact that Pa and Ma were charter members of the church meant they were deeply involved in the church's life. Pa really did go without new shoes one winter so he could contribute

to the buying of a church bell. That bell still rings in Walnut Grove, though it is in a Lutheran church now.

Also, there really was a Reverend E. H. Alden, whom Mrs. Wilder later wrote about in her books. He was the gentle minister who brought so much joy to the girls' lives by having sister churches in the East provide his fledgling church with gifts and a Christmas tree, the first one Laura had ever seen. Laura always loved the Christmas season and that was a special one, even though they themselves had so little to give.

As Laura noted in her books, the Reverend Alden was a much beloved man of God. He would have been their minister in De Smet, South Dakota, too, if a certain Edward Brown, a cousin of the radical abolitionist John Brown, had not appeared at the last minute with a letter purported to be from the district superintendent and indicating that he was to be the town's new minister. There is some question now about the authenticity of that letter of Reverend Brown's. But the deed was done.

The Reverend Alden moved on west, settling in Oregon. Meanwhile Laura was left to endure the long-winded, hellfire and damnation sermons of John Brown's cousin. Laura said she preferred the church's music to the sermons. She also admitted that she was rather uncomfortable with what people called "testimonies," which were often given on Wednesday nights. As she said years later, they offended her sense of privacy since she thought that loving God was like loving one's mother. You loved her, of course, but you didn't go around bragging about it.

Perhaps the biggest influence on Laura's religious life came from her pa and his devotion to the hymns of the church. Throughout her books are many references to the hymns they sang as Pa sat playing his fiddle at night by the open-hearth fire.

> *Rock of Ages, cleft for me,*
> *Let me hide myself in Thee. . . .*

These were the songs Laura Ingalls Wilder carried with her throughout life, ready companions of inspiration on the pilgrim journey.

❧

My little French Poodle, Incubus, is blind. . . . Of what he is thinking when he sits for long periods in the yard with his face to the sun I am too stupid to understand perfectly, but I feel that in his little doggy heart, he is asking the eternal "Why?" as we all do at times. After a while he seemingly decides to make the best of it and takes a walk around the familiar places or comes in the house and does his little tricks for candy with a cheery good will.

We are so accustomed to an abundance of fruit [on the farm] that we do not appreciate the fine cultivated sorts as we did the wild kinds that we gathered at the cost of much labor and discomfort. There is a moral here somewhere, and I will leave it for you to discover.

∾

The way of the land in the Ozarks [is that] we can farm three sides of the land, thus getting the use of many more acres than our title deeds call for.

∾

There is something in living close to the great elemental forces of nature that causes people to rise above small annoyances and discomforts.

∾

If patience and cheerfulness and courage . . . count for so much in man that he expects to be rewarded for them . . . surely such virtues in animals are worth counting in the sum total of good in the universe.

Down by the spring one morning
Where the shadows still lay deep,
I found in the heart of a flower
A tiny fairy asleep.

~

Now I know that spring is here, for as I passed the
little creek on my way to the mailbox, I saw
scattered papers caught on the bushes, empty
cracker and sandwich cartons strewn around on the
green grass, and discolored pasteboard boxes
soaking in the clear water of the spring. I knew then
that spring was here, for the sign of the picnickers
is more sure than that of singing birds and tender
green grass, and there is nothing more unlovely
than one of nature's beauty spots defiled.

~

A bird in a cage is not a pretty sight to me, but it is
a pleasure to have the wild birds and the squirrels
nesting around the house and so tame that they do
not mind our watching them. Persons who shoot or
allow shooting on their farms drive away a great
deal of amusement and pleasure with the game.

The joy of creation is soon swallowed up in dismay at the quick process of deterioration and decay.

∾

I know . . . that hawks are a benefit to farmers because they catch field mice and other pests, but I am sure they would not look for a mouse if there were a flock of chickens near by.

∾

Too many of the forests of the United States have been made into lumber even though there never has seemed to be lumber enough, and the waste of timber has been great. The great woods of the East and the North of our country have been destroyed.

∾

Ever the winds went whispering o'er the prairies,
Ever the grasses whispered back again,
And then the sun dipped down below the skyline
And stars lit just the outline of the plain.

2
Proper
Perspectives

Persons appear to us according to the light we
throw upon them from our own minds.

~

A good laugh overcomes more difficulties and
dissipates more dark clouds than any other one thing.

~

The way to success and a broad, beautiful outlook
on life more often than not leads over obstacles and
up a stiff climb before we reach the hilltop.

~

Why should we need extra time in which to enjoy
ourselves? If we expect to enjoy our life, we will have
to learn to be joyful in all of it, not just at stated
intervals when we can get time or when we have
nothing else to do.

~

Did you ever notice how hard it is to do our best if
we allow ourselves to become discouraged? If we are
disheartened, we usually lag in our efforts more or
less. It is so easy to slump a little when we can give
the blame to circumstances.

I never have been in favor of making good resolutions on New Year's Day just because it was the first day of the year. Any day may begin a new year for us in that way.

~

The uplift of a fearless heart will help us over barriers. No one ever overcomes difficulties by going at them in a hesitant, doubtful way.

~

No two persons see people and things alike. What we see and how we see depends upon the nature of our light.

~

Love at First Sight

~

When Laura Ingalls Wilder first saw the land that came to be called Rocky Ridge Farm, she loved the forty-acre unimproved woodlands as though they had been created especially for her. Indeed, it was Laura who implored her husband to take the place, for he saw more of the defects than the promise in what they were buying. She saw more of what the farm might be than what it had been.

Truth to tell, most of the money they had for the down payment had come from Laura herself. Almanzo had been so sick from the aftereffects of his 1888 stroke, he had only been able to catch an odd job now and then. Family was about the only form of social security in those days, and Laura faithfully worked ten hours a day for a dollar a day while Ma Ingalls took care of daughter Rose.

So in 1894, when Laura and Almanzo finally settled near the small town of Mansfield, Missouri, never to wander again, Laura had earned the right to see Rocky Ridge Farm through the "eyes of faith." To have seen the opportunity otherwise would have been to see forty acres of an Ozark hilltop, a log cabin hardly more livable than a chicken coop, five acres that had been set to apple trees, and a heavily wooded hillside unsuitable for anything but firewood. There was no barn, no workshop, no pen for the animals, and no animals to put in the pen.

Perhaps Mrs. Wilder loved the place (and continued to love it all her life despite its defects) because it was *hilltop* land near the very peak of the Ozarks. Having come from the rather bleak, treeless, and dry prairies, her new situation must have seemed like a delightful vision. Even the challenges would be different.

Frankly, most of Laura's prairie experiences had ended in bitter disappointment. Ma and Pa had not stayed even a full year in Kansas; the Minnesota prairies could grow a crop, but only the grasshoppers got to eat it; and in the Dakotas, you could see a promising harvest wiped out in a single hailstorm or baked to a crisp by a few weeks' dry weather. Out there, every tree had been a visual wonder and precious treasure.

Now Laura could claim a whole hillside full of trees, and they would plant even more, making room for one of the most impressive apple orchards of Wright County, Missouri. There never would be enough trees for Laura, and one of her last and greatest pleasures was to hire the only Mansfield taxi and go for drives through the Ozark autumns.

❧

We who live in the quiet places have the opportunity to become acquainted with ourselves, to think our own thoughts, and live our own lives.

❧

It does not so much matter what happens. It is what one does when it happens that really counts.

❧

My education has been what a girl would get on the frontier. I never graduated from anything and only attended high school two terms.

You are the window through which you must see
the world.

~

He came to a wall so high he feared his tiny horse
could not carry him over; but the fairy king said to
him, "Throw your heart over the wall, then follow
it!" So [the mortal] rode fearlessly at the wall, with
his heart already bravely past it, and went safely over.

~

To laugh and forget is one of the saving graces.

~

Let's be cheerful! We have no more right to steal
the brightness out of the day . . . than we have to
steal the purse of a stranger.

~

All good is for us if we but reach out our hand to
take it.

~

We are so likely to see defects in institutions close
at hand and imagine that farther away conditions
are so much better.

Several years before, this man had been seriously ill—there had been no hope of his living—but, to everyone's surprise, he had made a complete recovery, and, since then, he had always been remarkably happy and cheerful.

~

If we have a headache, we will forget it sooner if we talk of pleasant things.

~

If we wish to help make beauty and joy in the world, living in it and becoming lovely ourselves, we must follow the example of the lotus [flower] and strive toward light and purity into the sunshine of the good.

~

The things that people do would look so different to us if we only understood the reasons for their actions. . . . Even their sins might not look so hideous if we could feel what pressure and perhaps suffering had caused them.

Sometimes we realize our happiness only by comparison. It really appears true that "To appreciate heaven well/A man must have some fifteen minutes of hell."

~

To Be Thankful

~

*D*uring the course of her writing career, both as a journalist and as a book writer, Laura Ingalls Wilder had much to say on the topic of thankfulness. In her essays, she portrayed the attitude of thankfulness as a highly prized virtue that took notice of the common everyday things of life and held them to be of highest value. We might be thankful for a simple cup of cold water on a hot day. The reasons for being thankful did not have to be great because, for Mrs. Wilder, thankfulness was a quality that developed through the art of observation and mental comparison.

For example, sister Mary's blindness and its special meaning for Laura, who became Mary's eyes, is portrayed with great feeling and thoughtfulness in her eight children's books. In one episode, she poignantly explores the meaning of Mary's blindness and the unyielding silence of the universe on "the why?" of human suffering. She concluded that God was good—everybody knew that—but somehow Mary must know it in some special way. Even Mary admitted she didn't know how she knew it; she just *knew* it. And she knew that there were people even worse off than she was.

In a similar fashion Laura came to her own attitude of thankfulness through the struggles of her early-life setbacks and through her desire to make meaning out of it all.

At fifteen, she was a teacher and didn't want to be one.

At eighteen, she was married and a farmer's wife. Although she was glad to have Almanzo, she didn't want to be a farmer's wife.

At twenty-one, Laura found herself tied to a cripple who had tried to rush his recovery from diphtheria only to suffer a stroke. Almanzo would trip over boards and even small rocks and have to be helped up. He couldn't lift his legs high enough to climb steps. His energy, once unbounded, vanished quickly. His hands were so stiff he couldn't harness his own horses, let alone ride them. He who was only thirty-one walked with the shuffle of a decrepit old man. He was barely able to hold odd jobs around town.

With the farm slipping from the young family's grasp, Laura gave birth to another child. The boy, unnamed, died nine days later. A month later their farmhouse burned down, never to be rebuilt.

Laura was just twenty-two. She and her husband had

to live off the welfare of others. First a year in Minnesota with Almanzo's parents, then two years in Florida for a change of climate for "Manly's" legs, and finally two years back in De Smet.

Laura became a seamstress for a dollar a day. She hated sewing. For two years Almanzo and Laura struggled to earn one hundred dollars in savings so that they might leave the place of their sorrows.

In 1894, Laura was twenty-seven when they fled the Dakota prairies for good.

Bitter? Here is what Laura said later about the struggle of those days:

> The Man of the Place [has been] worried about the weather [of 1924]. He said the indications were for a dry season, and ever since I have been remembering droughts. There were dry years in the Dakotas when we were beginning our life together. How heartbreaking it was to watch the grain we had sown with such high hopes wither and turn yellow in the hot winds! And it was backbreaking as well as heartbreaking to carry water from the well to my garden and see it dry up despite all my efforts.
>
> I said at that time that thereafter I would sow the seed, but the Lord would give the increase, if there was any, for I could not do my work and

that of Providence also by sending the rain on the gardens of the just and the unjust.

Would that we all had the strength of character to trust God that much.

∽

Have you seen any fairies lately? I asked the question of a little girl not long ago. "Huh! There's no such thing as fairies," she replied. In some way the answer hurt me, and I have been vaguely disquieted when I have thought of it ever since. . . .
Have you seen any fairies lately, or have you allowed the harsher facts of life to dull your "seeing eye"?

∽

Blue is without doubt a heavenly color, [but] it is better in the skies than in one's mind.

∽

Did you ever take a little trip anywhere with your conscience easy about things at home, your mind free from worry, and with all care cast aside and eyes wide open? . . . You will be surprised how much adventure can enter into ordinary things.

"Oh, I have such a dreadful headache," we say and immediately we feel much worse. Our pain has grown by talking of it.

～

No one can become great who is not ready to take the opportunity when it comes.

3

Home
&
Family

Out in the meadow, I picked a wild sunflower, and,
as I looked into its golden heart, such a wave of
homesickness came over me that I almost wept. . . .
Across the years, the old home and its love called to
me, and memories of sweet words of counsel came
flooding back.

~

Blind Mary

~

*M*ary Amelia Ingalls, Laura's older sister, lost her
sight when she was fourteen. It would be nice to
think that Michael Landon's *Little House on the Prairie*
TV series was an accurate depiction of Mary's life after
that time, but it was not.

Generally, marriage was just "not in the cards" for
blind women back in those days. Certainly, the real Mary
never married and, it seems clear, was never asked. She
really did go to the blind school though. That wasn't made
up. In fact, there is still a school for the blind in Vinton,
a small town in eastern Iowa. The few records from that
time show Mary to have been a good and diligent student
who finished her course of study in something over five
years.

A sort of combination high school and college, the
Iowa School for the Blind taught both practical and

academic skills such as math, Braille, recitation, and domestic arts. Mary learned to make things out of beads, and her sewing went on unabated so long as someone selected the thread. There was moral training also, and Mary's teachers were impressed with her memory work in the Scriptures. Her large Braille Bibles are on display in De Smet.

After finishing school in 1889, Mary lived the rest of her life with Pa and Ma. She became a favorite aunt to Laura's daughter Rose. In fact, Mary avidly followed Rose's writing career, once remarking in a letter that Rose was the only family member to become famous.

Mary did not live to see herself immortalized in her sister's famous books. She died in 1928 at the age of sixty-three, just four years before Laura published her first stories about the soon-to-become-famous Ingalls family. Her death had not come as a complete surprise. Although Ma Ingalls lived to be eighty-four, when she died in 1924 the center of Mary's world seemed to collapse, and her own health failed rapidly thereafter.

Until recently, even within the last ten years, you could still talk to a few townspeople who remembered Ma and Mary as they walked every Sunday to the Congregational church that had so long been the center of their lives. But now, even those who knew them are gone.

Just as a little thread of gold, running through a fabric, brightens the whole garment, so women's work at home, while only the doing of little things, is like the golden gleam of sunlight that runs through and brightens all the fabric of civilization.

～

Such magic there is in Christmas to draw the absent ones home, and, if unable to go in the body, the thoughts will hover there! Our hearts grow tender with childhood memories and love of kindred, and we are better throughout the year for having, in spirit, become a child again at Christmastime.

～

Reading [a] message from my mother, I am a child again and a longing unutterable fills my heart for Mother's counsel, for the safe haven of her protection and the relief from responsibility which trusting in her judgment always gave me.

～

If the members of a home are ill-tempered and quarrelsome, how quickly you feel it when you enter the house. You may not know just what is wrong, but you wish to make your visit short.

If what has hitherto been woman's work in the world is simply left undone by them, there is no one else to take it up. If . . . their old and special work is neglected and only half done, there will be something seriously wrong with the world, for the commonplace home work of women is the very foundation upon which everything else rests.

~

Lessons learned at mother's knee last through life.

~

A woman's real business is the keeping of the house and caring for the family.

~

The kingdom of home, as well as the Kingdom of Heaven, is within.

~

A house built of lasting materials would be a much better monument to one's memory than a costly stone in a cemetery.

What is there in the attitude of your children
toward yourself that you wish were different?
Search your heart and learn if your ways toward
your own mother could be improved.

≈

Always in the springtime I want to build a house.

≈

[The] ideal home should be made by a man and
woman together.

≈

When to realms of boundless peace,
I am waiting to depart
Then my mother's song at twilight
Will make music in my heart.
"Hush, my babe, lie still and slumber;
Holy angels guard thy bed."
And I'll fall asleep so sweetly,
Mother's blessings on my head.

≈

Sometimes I wonder if the home ties would not be
stronger if our homes were built with more of an

idea of permanency. . . . A house, well built,
[should] last for generations.

~

Sisters Carrie and Grace

~

Caroline Celestia Ingalls, otherwise known as Carrie, was the only one of the girls actually to be born in a log cabin on the prairie—the Kansas prairie near the town of Independence, only fifteen miles away. Mary and Laura Ingalls were born in Wisconsin in what was even then relatively settled territory. The Ingalls family lived about a half-day's journey from Pa's parents.

These various distances are important only in the sense that they remind us that our concept of what is near and what is far has changed immensely with the advent of auto travel and improved roads. Even a short distance seemed like a long way to go when the roads were barely a path through the trees and the meeting of another traveler an unusual event.

So, although Carrie was born in a location that would today be nothing but a short drive from town, she really was a prairie child. The family's isolation was considerable in comparison with what we experience today. (Laura later wrote of the distance to Independence as though they had lived forty miles from it. She wasn't being untruthful; the

distance to civilization had seemed very great to her young perceptions.)

Grace Pearl Ingalls, the youngest Ingalls, was a pioneer daughter used to the limitless horizons of the prairie. Although she was born in a settled community in northern Iowa, the family soon made its trek to the new lands of the Dakota Territory. There is a story about Grace that is hard to believe, but may be true. She supposedly once asked sister Laura what a tree was, and Laura took out some paints and painted her a picture of a tree. The painting still survives and is on view at the Laura Ingalls Wilder Home and Museum in Mansfield, Missouri.

As the years rolled on, Carrie took up a career in journalism, working for many years right in the town of De Smet. She remained what was then called a spinster, wholly devoted to her career in journalism, and literally worked her way up from the bottom of the journalistic totem pole to become a full-fledged editor. Then, in her early forties, she met a widower named David Swanzey and gave up her career to be his wife and mother to his children.

Sister Grace also married and lived in and around De Smet all her life. Her husband, Nate, was a farmer, so she was already well-suited for the life she would lead. They had no children. At Grace's death in 1941, she left behind a short but wonderful diary that is available through the bookshops at each Ingalls home site, most prominent of which are the ones in De Smet and Mansfield. The diary

is a childhood one and records Grace's observations during the time shortly after Laura's marriage.

All the daughters seemed to have a gift with words.

～

Why not have a family motto? . . . If the motto of a family were, "My word is my bond," do you not think the children of that family would be proud to keep their word?

～

Marriage is not now the end and aim of [a woman's] existence.

～

Just come and visit Rocky Ridge [Laura and Almanzo's farm],
Please grant us our request;
We'll give you all a jolly time—
Welcome the coming; speed the parting guest.

$\frac{4}{\text{Work}}$
&
Play

I always have been a busy person, doing my own housework, helping the Man of the Place when help could not be obtained; but I love to work. And it is a pleasure to write. And, oh, I do just love to play!

~

The Time We Save

~

*L*aura Ingalls Wilder probably felt that the phrase "labor-saving devices" was among the most misguided in the English language. As for herself, Laura could only exclaim, "What labor saved!" During her ninety years of life, after all, she had gone from the horse-and-buggy era to the age of rocketry; in her experience, the new sewing machine, the new reaper, the new plow, the new tractor, the new car, and the new clothes washer weren't laborsaving devices. They were labormaking devices!

The new sewing machine only made it possible to do more mending. Now she could do twice as much in half the time, so she would use the *extra* time to raise more chickens. The new car made it possible to get out more often, so Laura became involved in more community work. The new tractor made it easier for Almanzo to plant more crops so, because farm labor never seemed available, Laura would turn a hand in the field.

Being a progressive woman, Laura was glad for each

new advance that enabled her to save a bit of time here and there. But being used to a full day and a busy schedule, she spent the time saved on civic betterment, church work, and doing good works, and then wondered ruefully what had become of the time she'd saved. What with keeping the books for a farm loan association, serving as an officer in the Eastern Star lodge, participating in the Athenians (a self-improvement club), and writing a woman's advice column, she was spending every bit of extra time each new device gave her, and then some.

Thus, it is no wonder, one discovers with a smile, that nearly a quarter of her columns over a period of fourteen years dealt either with worry and fret over too much work or offered still more advice on time management and correct priorities. Too much work and not enough play was a constant theme. But for those who might be getting off the hook by relaxing more than they should, Laura was ready with a worried scolding that they might be forgetting the value of laboring *six* days, as the Bible said, and only resting on *one*.

Mrs. Wilder well knew that it was one of the ironies of her life that, though living in one of the garden spots of the United States, she seemed unable to bring herself to schedule the necessary time to enjoy the time she'd saved.

∾

We may not "Remember the sabbath day to keep it holy," but we'll not forget to stop working.

~

I know a man who had a little patch of corn. He was not quite ready to cut it, and, besides, he said, "It is just a little green." He let it wait until the frost struck it, and now he says it is too dry and not worth cutting. The frost saved him a lot of hard work.

~

Mr. Barton used to be a Methodist preacher, [but] he thought perhaps he had made a mistake like the man who saw in a vision the letters GPC and thought he had a call to preach, the letters standing for "Go Preach Christ." Later he decided the letters meant "Go Plow Corn," so Mr. Barton made up his mind to follow the profession in which he excelled.

~

There has always been a great deal of misplaced pity for Adam because of his sentence to hard labor. . . . That was all that saved him after he was deported from paradise. It is the only thing that has kept his descendants as safe and sane as they are.

[Worry] almost makes one feel like the wife who called to the hired girl, "Liza Jane, come hurry and get up. This is wash day, and here it is almost six o'clock and the washing not done yet. Tomorrow is ironing day and the ironing not touched; next day is churning day and it's not begun, and here the week is half gone and nothing done yet."

~

In the Ozark hills, neglected ground will grow up to wild blackberry briars, loaded with fruit in season. As the shiftless old farmer said, "Anyone can raise blackberries if he ain't too durned lazy."

~

People used to have time to live and enjoy themselves, but there is no time anymore for anything but work, work, work.

~

I became an expert at the end of a cross-cut saw, and I still can "make a hand" in an emergency. Mr. Wilder says he would rather have me help than any man he ever sawed with.

I know from experience that it is very pleasant to have duty and inclination run hand in hand, and to be well paid in cash for doing right.

~

It takes judgment to plant seeds at the right time, in the right place, and hard digging to make them grow, whether in the vegetable garden or in the garden of our lives.

~

Oh, for a little time to enjoy the beauties around me! Just a little while to be free of the tyranny of things that must be done!

~

The Games Children Played

~

With the advent of television, and more recently with the profligate growth of electronic games, a whole class of person-to-person entertainment is about to pass from the familiar scenes of childhood. Children used to play what was commonly referred to as games— tag, cops and robbers, and cowboys and Indians (or to be more correct with the times: cowpersons and Native Americans).

Now children play with Nintendo and Sega, glued to a cathode-ray tube for hours, relating to cartoon characters by blasting them off the face of the screen. The technical skill of our sons and daughters is amazing. They can program our VCRs but still have trouble telling the time on a non-digital clock. They can score ten million points on a battery-run game, but reading bores them if there aren't any pictures and the text is too long.

Mrs. Wilder would have been astonished and alarmed. While she and her sisters were forced by their circumstances to spend a large part of their youth apart from other children and thus invented many solitary pleasures, when they did come finally to live near civilization, they were all the more eager to play and to organize games with their young neighbors.

Before the days of largely passive entertainment, children used to play a lot of games that involved footracing or just plain running. Their elders called it "letting off steam." Traditional running games, now largely disappeared, were such games as Fox and Geese, other various forms of tag, and the positively destructive Red Rover. ("Red Rover, Red Rover, send Billy on over." Then Billy would run from his team's side and try to crash through the interlocked arms of the other team. At all costs, the line must hold or Billy got to take a captive back to his team. That this game didn't produce a whole load of broken arms is testimony to the durability of young bones.)

But other games—indoor games—are also dropping from view: Thimble, Thimble, Who's Got the Thimble?, Drop the Handkerchief, and Drop the Clothes Pins into the Bottle. This last game could while away the hours. You stood on a good firm chair with a load of your mother's clothes pins and tried to drop them down the mouth of an empty milk bottle. To explain the attraction of this game to today's child is very difficult. First, you have to explain what clothes pins and a milk bottle are.

With these and other such simple pastimes, the young Laura and her friends would have passed the hours not spent in chores. Parents from Laura's childhood would have been absolutely amazed at the idea that one of their jobs was to entertain their children. "Why, you children must entertain yourselves!" they would have said—and they would have meant it.

∾

When we lived in South Dakota where the cold came early and strong, we once had a hired man who was a good worker, but whose money was too easily spent. In the fall when the first cold wind struck him, he would shiver and chatter and, always he would say, "Gee Mighty! This makes a feller wonder what's become of his summer's wages!"

Honest, well-directed labor need never descend
into drudgery.

❧

I am like the friend who was recovering from
influenza rather more slowly than is usually the
case. "I eat all right and sleep all right," said he. "I
even feel all right, but just the sight of a piece of
work makes me tremble."
"That," said I, "is a terrible affliction, but I have
known persons who suffer from it who never had
the influenza."

❧

Money hasn't any value of its own; it represents the
stored up energy of men and women and is really
just someone's promise to pay a certain amount of
that energy.

❧

A renter we once had was unable to plow the corn
in all summer. Before it rained, the ground was so
hard he could not keep the plow in, and besides, if
it did not rain, there would be no corn anyway, and
he believed it was going to be a dry season. When it
did rain, it was too wet to plow, and never was he

ready and able to catch that cornfield when the
ground was right for plowing.

≈

To be sure there are limits to the lessening of work.
I could hardly go so far as a friend who said, "Why
sweep? If I let it go today and tomorrow and the
next day, there will be just so much gained, for the
floor will be just as clean when I do sweep as it
would be if I swept every day from now until then."

≈

There is nothing wrong with God's plan that man
should earn his bread by the sweat of his brow.

≈

The Man of the Place, inquiring in town for help,
was told that it was not much use to look for it.
"Jack was in the other day and begged with tears in
his eyes for someone to come help him get in his
hay, and he couldn't get anyone." To be sure, the
sun was shining rather warm in the hay field and
the shade in the park was pleasanter.

We have so many machines and so many helps, in one way or another, to save time; and yet I wonder what we do with the time we save. Nobody seems to have any!

5
Virtues
&
Vices

To know that I have helped [someone] a little or made a day brighter will make my own work easier and cause the sun to shine on the dark days, for we all have them.

'Tis then a little place of sunshine in the heart helps mightily. And there is nothing that puts so much brightness there as having helped someone else.

≈

The tragedy of being unready is easy to find, for more often than not, success or failure turn upon just that one thing.

≈

The commands we give our children should be our translation of the laws of God and man founded on justice and the law of love, which is the Golden Rule.

≈

Our hearts are mostly in the right place, but we seem to be weak in the head.

≈

If there were a cry of "Stop, thief!" we would all stand still.

The safest course is to be as understanding as possible, and, where our understanding fails, to call charity to its aid.

～

A newcomer in the neighborhood says, "I do like Mrs. Smith! She seems such a fine woman." "Well, y-e-s," we reply. "I've known her a long time," and we leave the new acquaintance wondering what it is we know against Mrs. Smith. We have said nothing against her, but we have "damned her with faint praise."

～

The American pioneer spirit [is] of courage, jollity, and neighborly helpfulness.

～

Almanzo James Wilder:
The Mystery Man

～

Our modern picture of the Westerner is probably shaped by the fact that John Wayne made over seventy movies. Even a casual viewer is likely to have seen him in at least half a dozen westerns. Standing at six feet

four inches, he loomed large in the imagination and the reality of the screen. Invincible, heroic, larger than life.

Thus, it is with a bit of a shock that we realize the real Westerner, whether hero or bad man, stood in less heroic proportions: Kit Carson, scout and trailblazer, five feet six; Billy the Kidd, plenty tough at five feet four; Daniel Boone, woodsman and settler, five feet seven; and Almanzo James Wilder, the quiet hero who brought wheat to starving De Smet during the Long Winter, five feet four.

In perhaps only one way do the John Wayne films ring true to what is known of the real-life Westerner: These men, nearly all of them, were men of deeds rather than men of words. Others might elaborate or embellish what they did, but the men themselves seldom left behind records of their own feats. The popular phrase "the strong, silent type" well characterized most of them, just as it characterized John Wayne. Even Wyatt Earp didn't like to talk about the gunfight that made him famous.

Almanzo Wilder followed that pattern. He was Laura's husband, he farmed the land, he tinkered in his shop—and he didn't say much. Almanzo was certainly proud of his daughter, Rose, and of all her amazing accomplishments as a writer, but he seldom put pen to paper himself. We know nothing of what he thought of Laura's works, which immortalized him. Perhaps he was embarrassed.

While both mother and daughter could be volatile, Almanzo was a "live and let live" individual who held his tongue in check. No more comfortable in crowds than Laura, he could sit for hours and say not a word, whereas his wife could warm up and be the life of a gathering. She could speak readily about the major issues of the day, be they political, social, or religious. Not Almanzo. He didn't seem to care to express his opinions much. Some people might have thought him henpecked by both his wife and his daughter.

Certainly, Almanzo seemed more comfortable with men than with women. On the few days he did go into Mansfield each year, he always tried to stop in for a congenial chat at the service station where the business was never so brisk that you couldn't sit a spell and shoot the breeze. He liked to play an occasional game of pool at the downtown hall. He did have his friends, after all, and he was noted for his loyalty. But of the great many things we would like to know about him we have no record. He was just a silent man. Almanzo's strong stability in the face of early family crises served Laura and Rose very well. His record was in his deeds.

☙

There is something thrilling and ennobling in seeing a person brave death in a good cause, but to

watch anyone risk being butchered merely to make holiday sport savors too much of other things.

～

We are in the midst of a battle of standards of conduct and each of us is a soldier in the ranks.

～

I [have] thought seriously of cultivating a reputation for being peculiar, for, like charity, such a reputation seems to cover a multitude of sins.

～

It is a poor life that does not teach us to shed envy as a duck sheds raindrops.

～

Every good becomes evil when carried to excess.

～

Children get their bad tempers from their fathers; but we get our vanity from Adam, for we all have it, men and women alike.

～

Vices are simply overworked virtues.

People who pry into affairs which are none of their business consider the same actions disgraceful in others, and gossips think that they should be exempt from the treatment they give to other people. I never knew it to fail. It is very amusing at times to listen to the condemnation of others' actions by one who is even more guilty of the same thing.

~

We are all alike eager to lay upon someone else the blame for troubles that come from our own faults.

~

The real character of men and women comes to the surface under stress, and sudden riches is as strong a test as any.

~

We eat too much! Everyone says so! But we keep right on eating.

~

We heap up around us things that we do not need as the crow makes piles of glittering pebbles.

There are those who persistently disobey the laws of health, which, being nature's laws, are also God's laws, and then when ill health comes, wonder why they should be compelled to suffer.

∼

Life would be pleasanter, with some of the strain removed, if it were no longer true, as someone has said, that "things are in the saddle and rule mankind."

∼

We steal from today to give to tomorrow.

∼

Always there is a feeling of illness after indulging in a fit of temper.

∼

The way that is such an easy descent becomes, on return, a toilsome climb.

∼

The reputation of a careless spender is nothing to be desired.

No story is ever ended! It goes on, and on, and the effects of one followed [a] little girl all her life, showing her hatred of injustice.

~

Our motives are nearly always so mixed that it is easy to deceive ourselves.

$\dfrac{6}{\text{Wit}}$

Men are largely what their mothers have made them, and their wives usually finish the job.

❧

Few of us are bright enough to turn a slip to good account as did the schoolboy of long ago. This particular boy was late at school one icy winter morning, and the teacher reproved him and asked the reason for his tardiness.

"I started early enough," answered Tom, "but it was so slippery that every time I took one step ahead I slipped back two steps."

There was a hush of astonishment, and then the teacher asked, "But if that is true, how did you ever get here?"

"Oh, that's easy," replied Tom. "I was afraid I was going to be late and so I just turned around and came backward."

❧

[Farmers] hands are quite full . . . and it seems about the only way they could procure more help would be to marry more wives.

❧

Some time ago the semiannual house-cleaning was dropped from my program, very much to everyone's advantage. If a room needed cleaning out of season, I used to think "Oh, well, it will soon be house-cleaning time" and let it wait until then. I found I was becoming like the man who did "wish Saturday would hurry and come" so he could take a bath.

❧

The consumer wants something done about the high cost of living, but he wants all the benefit to accrue to himself.

❧

There is a touch of humor to be found in the fact that what we prepare for comes to us. . . . When the influenza came to our town, Mrs. C called a friend and tried to engage her to come and nurse her through the illness.

"Have you the influenza?" asked the friend. "Oh, no!" replied Mrs. C. "None of us has it yet, but I'm all ready for it. I have my bed all clean and ready to crawl into as soon as I feel ill. Everything is ready but a nurse, and I want you to come and take care of me."

In a very few days, Mrs. C was in bed with an attack of influenza. She had prepared for the visit, and she could say with [Job]: "The thing that I feared has come upon me."

The Man of the Place and I discovered the other day that we had, for some time, been saying to our friends, "Why don't you come over?" Can you think of a more awkward question than that? Just imagine the result if that question should always be answered truthfully! Some would reply, "Because I do not care to visit you."

~

Bright Laughter

~

Laura Ingalls Wilder probably inherited her sense of humor from her father. Pa Ingalls was a playful man who liked to get down on all fours and pretend he was a bear to scare and delight the young Mary and Laura. More than Ma, he was the storyteller in the family, and it was to preserve some of Pa's family stories that Laura set out to write *Little House in the Big Woods* in 1931.

When she was not writing about her father's antics, Laura liked best to tell stories on herself. Three stories from childhood particularly stuck in her memory.

One story she liked to tell on herself was her devious plot to get even with Nellie Oleson for a slight Nellie had given, out of hearing of the elders, to Laura's parents. Laura was so incensed by this that she could hardly wait to lure the unsuspecting Nellie to her house for a party

just so she could trick Nellie into wading in nearby Plum Creek.

Once she had Nellie wading in the water, she teased a large crawdad out from under a rock and commenced to get Nellie hysterically frightened that she would have her toes bitten off. An extra pleasure was the fact that Nellie got leeches attached to her and these little bloodsucking animals had to be pulled off, which only added to Nellie's discomfort. Yes, Laura could "dish it out" as well as take it, and she knew she should have been sorry, but she never quite lost her delight in telling the story.

Another story she liked to tell that puts her in a more humane light was one that involved the Thanksgiving meal that never was.

While living near Silver Lake, and before other settlers had begun to arrive, Pa said he would take his gun and get them a nice fat goose for Thanksgiving. Almost immediately, as children will, there arose a dispute on what sort of stuffing should fill the not-shot-but-soon-to-be-shot goose. The choices were dressing with sage (Mary) and dressing without sage (Laura). The dispute waged hot and heavy—with Ma having to intervene—until Pa came home without any goose at all!

Laura liked to say afterward, about the lesson learned, that she would have been glad for goose without *any* stuffing if Pa had only returned with one.

Another story Laura liked to tell was not about

herself but about cousin Charley, Pa's brother's son. The family had already begun to decide that Charley was going to turn out bad because he was so ornery and disobedient to his elders.

Once, while Pa and his brother cut hay with great curving scythes, Charley played around at the edge of the pasture. Then he started a game on the men. He would suddenly shriek out a cry like there was something wrong, and both men would drop the scythes and come running, only to find Charley laughing at them because he had tricked them. After a couple of experiences like this, the men stopped coming at Charley's cries. The only thing was, Charley wouldn't stop yelling and jumping, so the men finally dropped their scythes again, prepared to have Charley laugh at them. But this time, Charley had actually stumbled into a nest of hornets. It was a long time before Charley was up to any mischief again.

Laura's only remark years later was that Charley had turned out a lot better than expected.

∾

Never yet have I been "stumped."

∾

The small boy gave the hen [some advice]. When he heard her wildly cackling to announce that she had

67

laid an egg, he exclaimed, "Aw, shut up! What's the use of making such a fuss? You couldn't help it!"

～

"Now I have no tact whatever, but speak plainly," said [my friend] pridefully. "The Scotch people are, I think, the most tactful, and the Scotch, you know, are the trickiest nation in the world." As I am of Scotch descent, I could restrain my merriment no longer, and when I recovered enough to say, "You are right, I am Scotch," she smiled ruefully and said, "I told you I had no tact."

～

Most furniture, especially that in the bedroom . . . is just high enough from the floor to permit dust and dirt to gather underneath but not high enough to be cleaned easily.

～

"How do you fellows [sitting under the park's shade trees] pass the time here all day? What do you do to amuse yourselves?"

A man emptied his mouth of its accumulation of tobacco juice and replied in a lazy drawl, "Oh, we jest set and—think—and—sometimes—we—jest—set."

❧

One free show was shocking. I never had watched while knives were thrown around a human target. The target, as usual, was a woman, and a man threw the knives.

❧

I have at last found the good in a hard spell of illness. It is the same good the Irishman found in whipping himself.
"Why in the world are you doing that?" exclaimed the astonished spectator.
"Because it feels so good when I stop," replied the Irishman with a grin.

❧

Is there something in life you want very much? Then pay the price and take it, but never expect to have a charge account and avoid paying the bills.

A certain judge adjourned without observing the proper formalities, and, when one of the lawyers protested, exclaiming, "You can't do that! You can't do that!" the judge replied: "Well, by ———— I have done it!"

≈

Sometimes I wonder if telephones and motor cars are altogether blessings. . . . When [my neighbor] gets into her car, it is almost sure to run for twelve to fifteen miles before she can stop it, and that takes it way down the road past me.

≈

[As] the schoolboy described in his essay on pins—"Pins has saved many lives by not swallering of 'em."

≈

I never knew anyone to be ready for cold weather in the fall or for the first warm spell in the spring.

Oh, the shops of Chinatown! I do not understand how any woman could resist their fascination.

~

An infidel asserted that he would not believe anything that he could not see. It was a good retort the Quaker made, "Friend! Does thee believe thee has any brains?"

~

A man of my acquaintance used to complain bitterly to his wife because she did not make enough slop in the kitchen to keep a hog. "At home," he said, "they always kept a couple of hogs, and they did not cost a cent, for there was always enough waste and slop from the kitchen to feed them." How ridiculous we all are at times! This man actually thought something was wrong instead of being thankful that there was no waste from his kitchen!

~

I should like to know who designed our furniture as we use it today. It must have been a man. No

woman . . . who has the care of a house would ever
have made it as it is.

~

[A] renter was always ready to take advantage of his
opportunities. His horses would break into the
cornfield at night, or were turned in (we never knew
which), and in the fall when the Man of the Place
wanted a share of what corn was left, he was told
that the horses had eaten all his share!

7
Nation
&
Society

A nation can be no greater than the sum of the greatness of its people.

~

If we, the people, hold fast to and live by beautiful ideals, they are bound to be enacted by our government, for, in a republic, the ideas of the people reach upward to the top instead of being handed down.

~

I really think that a training in public speaking and an understanding of public questions would be worth more to pupils of the schools than games of basketball.

~

I protect myself without calling on the government at Washington. I do for myself at least as much as I can.

~

Think for Yourself

~

*I*f Mrs. Wilder didn't actually hate the growth of Big Government, she came close to it. Long before it was fashionable to complain about Washington and too much Big Brother government, Laura Ingalls Wilder was urging people to be "independent," to think for themselves, and to do without government assistance and advice.

Laura was not by any means reacting to Roosevelt's New Deal legislation. She was decrying big government in the twenties under conservative presidents like Harding and Coolidge. Perhaps Mrs. Wilder was irked at the federal government because so often it was the farmers and agricultural workers (the "hicks") who were the target of well-meaning welfare and "good advice."

The precursor to today's U.S. Department of Agriculture was always sending out helpful pamphlets extolling the virtues of common cleanliness and good hygiene, apparently under the impression that farmers were generally unkempt rubes and hayseeds. Such snobbery drove Mrs. Wilder to distraction.

One government tract that particularly annoyed Laura was one that told how farmers should care for their leather shoes by oiling them to keep the leather soft and pliable. "Clean your shoes every day and keep the mud off them" was the sage advice. Mrs. Wilder took umbrage at the thought that farm people might have lost their common sense and actually be in need of advice to clean their shoes!

With pride, Laura pointed out that during the "Hard Winter" of 1880–81, the stranded homesteaders of De Smet, South Dakota, had learned how to make bread by using their coffee grinders as flour mills to grind their

remaining supply of seed wheat into flour for baking. Additionally, the unadvised homesteaders had learned how to twist plain prairie hay into "wood sticks" for their stoves because there was no wood or coal.

Mrs. Wilder felt that people lost a great deal when they lost the ability to adapt and learn how to think and do for themselves. There was a satisfaction in personal initiative that couldn't be beat. She feared that a "helpful" government might take away that spirit of initiative.

∾

The good still rises over the bad in the hearts of humanity.

∾

No one is giving a thought to the fact that in a free, democratic world, power will be in the hands of women.

∾

We accept, without thinking about it, the fact that happy nations do not appear in history.

Keep up with the march of progress, for the time is coming when the cities will be the workshops of the world . . . while real cultural, social, and intellectual life will be in the country.

That which is the wonder of one age is the commonplace of the next.

~

We go from achievement to achievement, and no one knows the ultimate heights the human race may reach.

~

Our next president should be chosen for his fitness for the place as though we were hiring him to attend to our own private business.

~

Everyone these days has a try at telling what is wrong with business conditions. One thing causing us a great deal of trouble and making much higher the high cost of living is the extra price we pay for fancy packages.

Nearly all writers and thinkers are looking for a new order, a sort of social and industrial revolution.

~

When we are tempted to be impatient and too critical of our leaders, we might think, as I heard a woman say, "Few of us would have their jobs." . . . Let's root for our leaders now and then.

~

Events of greatest importance are least noticed, even while they are occurring under our very eyes.

~

A friend writes me of New York, "I like it and I hate it. There's something you've got to love, it's so big—a people hurrying everywhere, all trying to live and be someone or something—and then when you see the poverty and hatefulness, the uselessness of it all, you wonder why people live here at all."

~

A "government of the people, for the people and by the people" can be no better than the people.

We must get rid of the habit of classing all women
together politically and thinking of the "woman's
vote" as one and indivisible.

~

Of Men and Women

~

Sometimes it is supposed the "battle of the sexes," as
it has been called, has only erupted into outright
warfare in recent times. Perhaps there is a grain of truth
to this, but if so, preparations for the battle were in the
making a long time ago.

Laura Ingalls Wilder certainly saw the warfare coming.

For example, *feminism* is a word with which the
young Mrs. Wilder would have been thoroughly familiar.
The word and its personification were brought back from
the East by Laura's sister-in-law, the famous "Lazy, lousy,
'Liza Jane" Wilder from *Little Town on the Prairie*.

Eliza Jane Wilder was what was known as a "bachelor
girl" of the 1880s. As the frontier pushed westward,
women had steadily seen a sort of ever-expanding liberation of their own lives as they ceased to be merely house
decorations and increasingly took their places beside their
men in hewing out a life on the frontier.

Women like Eliza Jane Wilder, who only a generation before would have been called "old maids," now

ventured forth to settle on homestead claims of their own. They were given no preference over the men, but neither were they discriminated against. According to the Homestead Act of 1862, if a person, either male or female, could endure the loneliness and "improve" the land, the land became theirs after five years.

In fact, Eliza Jane Wilder did prove up on her claim, but then found the life of a settler so rugged and lonely that she sold it and moved east to work at a government job in Washington, D.C. Washington, then much more of a large town than a city, was full of women just like Eliza who were seeking their fortunes on their own and not about to let their gender get in the way. There she found liberating company and a free flow of ideas among the other bachelor women of the town.

Years later, when a still-unmarried Eliza Jane left her job and returned home to live with her parents, her newfangled ideas didn't faze either her mother or Laura, who was living with her in-laws while Almanzo struggled to regain his health following his bout with diphtheria.

The long hours Eliza Jane Wilder spent in seeking to convert her mother to feminist views only seemed to amuse Laura. She could see that her mother-in-law, Angeline Day Wilder, had little use for such imported ideas. Angeline already was a liberated woman so far as Angeline was concerned. On the farm, she was her husband's partner in every sense of the word. Having already successfully raised six children, she continued to raise produce for market and consulted about the general business of the place on an equal footing with her husband. James Mason Wilder wouldn't have made a decision without her.

True, child rearing had been Angeline's main job. But after a relatively short period of time, the boys were apprenticed to work with their father, and Angeline was free to guide her daughters into useful pursuits such as butter and egg production and cloth weaving. It was useless to talk of liberation to a woman who probably already felt too busy and liberated as it was.

Laura observed Angeline and Eliza Jane's conversations, and the experience led her to develop a theory as to why divorce seemed so much higher in the city than it did in the country. As Laura saw it, the difference had to do with work. In the city, husbands and wives might well find that their work led them into competitive situations, whereas on a farm, *both* husband and wife *had* to work *together* or neither one could make a go of it.

This idea of working for a common goal appealed to Laura, who felt that in the end, a husband and wife working side by side as equals could only strengthen a marriage.

For the cruel child to become a hard-hearted boy
and then a brutal man is only [his] stepping along
the road on which he has started.

∼

In these days when we feed those who are not
hungry, we are stealing from those who are starving,
even though the food is our own.

∼

Following all the unrest and unreason on down to
its real source where it lurks in the hearts of people,
its roots will be found there in individual
selfishness. . . . There is no oppression of a group of
people but that which has its roots and inception in
the hearts of the oppressors. There is no wild
lawlessness and riot and bloodlust of a mob but that
which has its place in the hearts and of the persons
who are that mob.

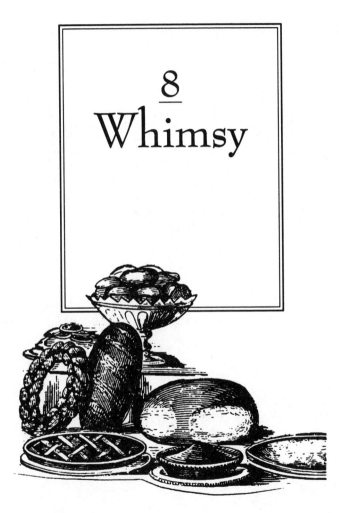

$\frac{8}{}$
Whimsy

It is better to make a good pie than a poor poem.

~

Washing in buttermilk will whiten the hands and face.

~

The green country boy [had] never seen a carpeted floor. A new family moved in and this boy went to the house one day. As he started to enter the door, he saw the carpet . . . swung his long arms and jumped clear across the small room, landing on the hearth. Turning to the astonished woman of the house, he exclaimed: "Who Mam! I mighty nigh stepped on your kiverled [bedspread]!"

~

A child's craving for sweets is a call of nature. It is necessary to the proper development of their bodies.

~

Bring yourself up to date.

~

While looking over the pages of a catalog advertising articles from 2 cents to 10 cents, the Man of the Place said, "There are a good many little tricks you'd like to have. Get what you want; they will only cost a few cents." So, I made out a list of what I wanted, things I decided I could not get along without. . . .

I was surprised when I added up the cost to find that it amounted to $5. I put the list away intending to go over it and cut out some things to make the total less. That was several months ago, and I have not yet missed any of the things I would have ordered. I have decided to let the list wait until I do.

~

[Women] have been privileged to look on and criticize the way the world has been run. "A man-made world" we have called it now and then, implying that women would have done so much better in managing its affairs. The signs indicate that we are going to have a chance to remake it nearer to the heart's desire. I wish I might be sure that we would be equal to our opportunity.

~

Rhubarb and tomatoes will remove stains from the fingers.

~

Then there is the gasoline engine. Bless it! . . . It can be made to do the pumping of the water and

the churning, turn the washing machine, and even run the sewing machine.

~

The fact is that while there has been a good deal of discussion for and against women in business, farm women have always been businesswomen—and I have never heard a protest.

~

Common Fare

~

*F*ood is one of life's great pleasures, so we may be tempted to wonder how our pioneer forbears did without it. Did without food? Well, maybe not. But how did they do without *healthy food?* That's another question.

Salted meats. The phrase doesn't sound as good as salted peanuts, but you were fortunate indeed to have meat "salted away" for the winter. Freshly butchered meat (and you did the butchering) was placed in a wooden trough with a drain hole. As the meat dried and drained, it was layered with salt—pounds of it.

After the meat was properly "cured," it hung in a naturally cold place till it was needed. Maybe old-timers didn't eat enough cured meat to hurt them, since whatever was stored had to be made to last the winter. Still, when they did have meat, it was as salty as brine. If we'd ever sat down to a meal with great, great Grandpa William and great, great Grandma Alice, we'd have run for the water pitcher first thing. Maybe it helped that they didn't know that much salt was bad for them.

Lard. You could hardly do any essential thing in the kitchen without it. If you wanted to fry a piece of salt meat—who had ever heard of baked or broiled?—you put some lard in the skillet and then browned the meat well on both sides (nothing about cooking meat rare or medium in those days). And fried chicken—why, all the best recipes were laced with lard! You almost wanted enough lard to cook the chicken like French fries. Indeed, fried potatoes were a staple—cooked in lard, of course.

All of the best pie crusts and baked things were made with lard. In fact, you probably have not had a good pie until you've had one with a crust made with lard. Breads, donuts, and cakes were made the same way.

Butter. A young man of my acquaintance, newly married, was once sent to the store by his young bride for butter. The young innocent was foolish enough to bring back real butter when she had meant margarine. There was no problem like that in the old days. Butter was good for you. A simple breakfast meal was buttered toast and mush. Lunch and supper usually came with bread and butter too. Now, if you have bread with your meals, there is a very real danger that it might be *healthy* bread with a butter substitute.

Sugar. The best for last. Back then, sugar was thought to be absolutely essential to a growing child's

health: a nutritious food. On this, both the dentists and the parents agreed. Medicines, Mary Poppins assures us, were taken with a whole spoonful of sugar. That, no doubt, helped in the swallowing of about anything.

One recipe of the time, included in the book *I Remember Laura,* calls for twenty-four cups of sugar to make a few quarts of gooseberry conserve (although this is no wonder since gooseberries are quite sour). Many candies were of a marzipan-like quality and only palatable because of the sugar, and pancakes and syrup were a regular breakfast for farmhand and banker alike.

Everybody ate well in those days, with a free and easy conscience, because they knew for a fact that what they were eating was good for them!

∿

A tea made from garden sage will darken the hair and help it grow.

∾

The city woman works outside her home, her business interests and occupations pull away from the home life and from marriage.

∾

The remedy for the evils of high prices is increased production.

The hair should not be washed too often, for this will cause it to fall [out].

~

Anyone you meet will tell you there is no time for anything anymore.

~

The idea of a woman's party, a political division on sex lines, is distasteful to women.

~

Common table salt is one of the best tooth powders.

~

A band of Spanish adventurers came up the Mississippi River and wandered through the Ozarks. Somewhere among the hills they hid their treasure in a cave, and it never has been discovered to this day.

~

The vagaries of a foolish sitting hen will relieve the monotony for [an] entire day!

9
Gazing Forward . . . Looking Back

As far back as I can remember, the old times were
good times. They have been good all down
through the years, full of love and service, of
ideals and achievement—the future is ours to
make it what we will.

❧

Let us make [memories] carefully of all good things,
rejoicing in the wonderful truth that while we are
laying up for ourselves the very sweetest and best of
happy memories, we are at the same time giving
them to others.

❧

My childish memories hold the sound of the war
whoop, and I see pictures of painted Indians.

❧

Did you ever hear anyone say, "I don't know what
the world is coming to. . . . Things were different
when I was young." That remark has become a
habit with the human race, having been made at
least 900 years ago.

Beginning Again

~

"It was easier in the old days." That's a phrase we've all heard at some time or other, usually from someone who is fondly recalling a not-too-accurately remembered past.

But maybe it really was easier in the old days, in at least one significant respect. It was easier to fail—utterly, miserably, completely, financially—and simply start all over again. Yes, maybe you did have to pack up your belongings on short notice and leave in the middle of the night, as Ma and Pa Ingalls and the children had to do once. (Laura *didn't* write about *that* episode in her books.) That was back in Burr Oak, Iowa, where the family had spent a difficult two years with virtually nothing to show for it in the end except the few transportable belongings they got away with. A Mr. Bisbee lost a couple of months rent, but no sheriff went after the Ingallses and Mr. Bisbee got his rental back in usable condition. The fact is, Pa lost money in about the same way when the man who bought his log cabin near Lake Pepin, Wisconsin, gave up pioneering and went back east, probably unable to make his payments.

Small businessmen and farmers took their losses back then with no safety net. Nor was it a big disgrace if a person defaulted only once or twice on his debts, because nearly everyone else had done so too. Bankers took their

chances. Money was loaned at about 10 percent in the 1880s, but there was no Federal Deposit Insurance Corporation for savings accounts. So it wasn't unusual for banks to end up owning land they didn't want and then fail because of their own debt load. Banks weren't trusted the way they are today. The old joke about keeping your money in a sock or under the mattress was quite true. People who did that were better off than those who lost everything during a bank panic.

The good thing was, there was just enough going on in terms of business at each new town sprouting from the prairie that a jack-of-all-trades like Pa Ingalls could recover pretty quickly. Broke in 1878, he was a well-paid railway clerk in 1879 with enough money and credit to establish another farm, be elected to a public office in the brand-new town of De Smet, and buy a lot in town that he later sold at a profit. Thereafter, De Smet was always busy enough to provide Charles Ingalls with carpentry work or a position as an insurance agent. The home he built in De Smet still stands, a museum now.

Common misfortunes created a camaraderie of rugged understanding: Though a man's credit may not have been good two years ago, it was what he was good for *today* that counted. If people never felt entirely safe from the wolf at the door, they did get used to hearing him scratch around on the doorstep and learned to sleep through it.

It is necessary that we dream now and then. No one ever achieved anything from the smallest to the greatest unless the dream was dreamed first.

～

I think there is no great gain without a little loss. [Almanzo and I] do not carry water from the spring anymore, which is a very great gain, but it was sometimes pleasant to loiter by the way—and that we miss a little.

～

Even though one is not in the habit of making New Year's resolutions, to be broken whenever the opportunity arises, still, as the old year departs, like Lot's wife, we cannot resist a backward glance. As we see in retrospect the things we have done that we ought not and the things we have left undone that we should have done, we have a hope that the coming year will show a better record.

～

To me, it is a joy that "no man knoweth what a day may bring forth," and that life is a journey from one discovery to another. It makes of every day a real adventure; and if things are not to my liking

today, why, "There's a whole day tomorrow that ain't tetched yet," as the old man said.

～

The days never have been long enough to do the things I would like to do. Every year has held more of interest than the year before.

～

When men or women have advanced, they do not go back. History does not retrace its steps.

～

No one can really welcome the first gray hair or look upon the first wrinkles as beautiful.

～

We cannot take our opinions from our fathers nor even keep the opinions we formed for ourselves a few years ago. Times and things move too fast.

～

A year of being crippled has taught me the value of my feet, and two perfectly good feet are now among my dearest possessions.

Sometimes we are inclined to wish our childhood days might come again, but I am always rescued from such folly by remembering a remark I once heard a man make: "Wish I were a boy again! I do not! When I was a boy I had to hoe my row in the cornfield with father and the hired man . . . then, while they rested in the shade, I had to run and get the drinking water."

≈

The world seems a lonesome place when mother has passed away and only memories of her are left.

≈

I have learned that few persons have such happy and successful lives that they would wish to spend years in just remembering.

≈

We must first see the vision in order to realize it; we must have the ideal or we cannot approach it. But when once the dream is dreamed, it is time to wake up and "get busy." We must "do great deeds, not dream them all day long."

There is no turning back nor standing still; we must go forward into the future, generation after generation, toward the accomplishment of the ends that have been set for the human race.

~

They Didn't Know

~

*T*he events of history, even personal history, often depend on small things. On the whole, it has to be said that the family of Charles Philip Ingalls never prospered in any significant way other than in the intangible way their family life held them together through thick and thin, through good times and bad.

The Ingallses' family life, where it related to establishing a solid financial footing, was often a case of "if we had only known."

When Pa moved to Kansas Territory, he moved too far and located on Indian land that the government, in one of its few truthful pacts with the Indians, really did intend to remain Indian land. (Later on, the government reneged again on a promise made to the Indians, but by then it was too late for Pa and Ma.) Charles Ingalls spent less than a year in Kansas, not even harvesting one crop before he had to move on or be kicked out by the government—*his* government.

Similarly, Pa couldn't have known about the vagaries of the weather. You judged new territory by what you saw when you first got there and things hadn't been ruined by too many settlers doing exactly the same thing you were doing—looking for the last new beginning that was going to make your family's fortune.

That's what everybody that moved in to settle the little town of De Smet, South Dakota, got caught by too. The weather. It fooled them.

The land was all right. It was good for plowing, incredibly fertile, and not a tree to cut down or burn out anywhere. The fertile prairie lay before each homesteader as a bright promise for a better life than the hardscrabble years of the past. Except for the weather.

There was no Willard Scott to tell Mr. Ingalls and all the others that they were walking right into a big trap. The National Weather Service wasn't there to tell them that South Dakota was and is a dryland farming state. You've got to grow things a certain way and plant only certain crops or you won't make it at all.

Two years of above-average rainfall greeted the hardy pioneers as they began to stake out claims in the new Dakota Territory. That good weather was just enough to get them started—and in debt—when the real, normal rainfall returned.

Naturally, the settlers around De Smet couldn't understand it. Why drought? Why now, of all times? But

it wasn't drought at all. It was just their misfortune to be caught on marginal farmland. The government, in its own sincere ignorance, even tried to encourage claim holders to develop tree claims on land that had never naturally been hospitable to any tree. You can even go to De Smet now and find a few trees that Pa Ingalls and Almanzo Wilder planted before the "drought" finally drove them off the land—Almanzo and Laura heading south for Missouri, and Pa moving the rest of his family to town where he lived out his days as a carpenter and odd-job worker.

The broken dreams weren't their fault. They just didn't know. Pioneer fortitude *had* to carry them through such cruel, ironic things. The pioneers didn't have much choice about it.

❧

Youth ever gazes forward while age is inclined to look back. And so older persons think things were better when they were young.

❧

What they bought were possibilities and the chance of working out their dreams.

I could ride. I do not wish to appear conceited, but
I broke my own ponies. Of course, they were not
bad, but they were broncos.

~

Melancholy old age will not come upon those who
refuse to spend their time indulging in dreams of
the past.

10
Wisdom

Life begins at eighty.

≈

There are just as many hours in the day as ever, and
. . . there is time enough for the things that matter
if time is rightly used.

≈

By the sacrifice we make in giving we show our love
for humanity, our pity for the helpless, and our
generosity toward those less fortunate than ourselves.

≈

So much depends on starting . . . children right!

≈

It is the lack of Christianity that has brought us
where we are. Not a lack of churches or religious
forms but of the real thing in our hearts.

≈

We are too much like the woman who boycotted eggs
because they were too high and then, without a
protest, paid $36 for a pair of low shoes. . . . It is so
easy to throw away with one hand what we save with
the other.

Invisible forces are all about us. Of some we have an imperfect knowledge while of others we have as yet only the vaguest ideas.

~

A dentist once said to me, "I don't care whether people come to me when they should or put off coming as long as they possibly can. I know they'll come in time, and the longer they put it off the bigger my bill will be when they do come." We begin to pay the dentist when our teeth first need attention whether they have that attention or not.

~

There is still room for improvement in children's clothes. They are much too fussy to be either beautiful or becoming. Why trouble with fancy, changeable children's styles? There will be plenty of time for them to learn all the vanities of dress later.

~

An opinion supported by a good reason, kindly stated, should not offend.

However fleeting and changeable life may appear to be on the surface, we know that the great underlying values of life are always the same; no different today than they were a thousand years ago.

~

[We] go lightheartedly on our way never thinking that by a careless word or two we may have altered the whole course of human lives, for some persons will take [our] advice and use it.

~

[It is] the inalienable right of a child to have something of his very own.

~

Cooperation is the keynote of affairs today, and our lives seem to be governed mostly by the advice of experts. [But] the more we think for ourselves, the less we shall need advice; and high-priced experts would not need to waste . . . our money in telling us things we should think out for ourselves.

~

Sometimes we recognize as a special blessing what heretofore we have taken as a matter of course.

When we recover from a serious illness, just a
breath drawn free from pain is a matter for rejoicing.

~

We may have almost anything in the world if we are
willing to pay the price.

~

Caroline Lake Quinter Ingalls

~

*M*any people know by now that there was a strange
dynamic that went into the writing of Laura Ingalls
Wilder's pioneer saga. Daughter Rose did the finishing
work on the stories while Laura supplied the straight
narrative and the facts upon which all of the stories are
strung together. Mother and daughter worked together,
but sometimes at cross-purposes.

Perhaps the depiction of Laura's mother is one place
where the usually successful dynamic broke down. Some
people have thought this because it is always Ma Ingalls
who is trying to put a brake on the wandering foot of her
husband, Charles. It is often Ma who seems to fret and
worry over each new situation; Pa is the optimist. Ma
doesn't like Indians—in fact, she is downright prejudiced
about them. When Laura begins to date Almanzo it is Ma
who is disapproving; Pa says he'd trust Almanzo anywhere.

But how much of this is really true? After all, Caroline was born of pioneer stock too. She did not come out to the West as some eastern bride unprepared for the rugged frontier. She and Pa were born to the same stations in life.

There is at least some evidence that Caroline Ingalls's caution was born out of good common sense. If Pa really was the dreamer of the family, always wanting to move on to new places, it might well have been that Caroline understood they would likely be no more successful in a new place than they had been in the place they'd just left. After all, Pa's track record at sticking to any one activity or location had not been all that good up to the time that Ma purportedly put her foot down and said that De Smet, South Dakota, was as far as they would go.

Nor does it appear, according to the bare facts, that Ma was any more prejudiced about the Indians than was anyone else at the time. Stories that circulate outside the "canon" of Laura's books show Ma to have been just as brave and sensible as Pa when it came to dealing with "hostile" Native Americans. At least one account gives *her* the credit for keeping the family from getting scalped in Indian Territory!

As for her initial doubts about Almanzo's intentions, it is hard to know what Ma really thought. Laura was the first daughter to get married, and frontier towns didn't have an oversupply of reputable males. Indeed, Almanzo was ten

years Laura's senior when he began courting her (she was sixteen). Since Almanzo was a settler, too, and subject to the same hardships as other settlers, Ma might have been concerned that her daughter was getting no more advantage at the start of her life than she had. About that, Ma Ingalls proved quite correct.

❧

A man is perhaps slower to adapt himself to new things than a woman.

❧

Children should be made to obey or shown that to disobey brings punishment. Thus, they will learn the lesson every good citizen and every good man and woman learns sooner or later—that breaking a law brings suffering.

❧

It is not vanity to wish to appear pleasing . . . nor is it a matter of small importance. To be well groomed and good to look at will give us an added self-respect and a greater influence over others.

112

If we are such bad company that we can't live with ourselves, something is seriously wrong . . . for sooner or later we shall have to face ourselves alone.

∼

It means much to a child . . . to be an honest winner or a good loser in whatever contest he takes part.

∼

There is an old maxim which I have not heard for years nor thought of in a long time. "To sweep a room as to God's laws makes that, and the action, fine."

$\dfrac{11}{\text{Life}}$
$\&$
Truth

The true way to live is to enjoy every moment as it
passes, and surely it is in the everyday things
around us that the beauty of life lies.

~

Compensations

~

*A*lmanzo always said there were compensations.
Laura's husband observed that the rich had their
ice during the summer, but the poor had theirs during the
winter. He would have known.

When Almanzo James Wilder was a boy, he grew up
on a prosperous grain, sheep, and cattle farm in upstate
New York. In fact, Malone, New York, is so far north it
is almost in Canada. Every winter the Wilders harvested
ice from their frozen ponds, carted it to their block house,
insulated the ice with sawdust, and closed the building very
tightly against the summer heat.

This kind of preservation worked wonderfully. A
well-insulated building could keep ice through most of the
hottest weather; sometimes there was ice for the fall. Thus,
the well-to-do Wilders had their ice in both winter *and*
summer.

However, this hard-won prosperity did not carry over
even into Almanzo's generation. For one thing, the
Wilder family was just too large for there to be a great

distribution of wealth. And as it was, no son inherited the family farm anyway. Almanzo's older brother, Royal, wanted to be a storekeeper and kept to that goal all his life. As for Almanzo, he headed west—to be his own boss and make it on his own—as soon as his father gave permission. Apparently neither son wanted to be "beholdened" to his father.

Almanzo was young for a homestead settler, but he figured it wasn't his age that mattered to Uncle Sam, but whether he was willing to work and maintain his hold on his own claim. After five years, if Almanzo had made improvements to his property, he got the land "free" and clear.

And Almanzo did "prove out" on his claim. In fact, he added even more land to his acreage when he became Laura's husband. He wanted to show his new wife, not just Uncle Sam, that there was prosperity in farming. Manly, as he was called, hoped to prove to Laura, who was skeptical, that they could make a go of it in only three years.

Well, Almanzo finally did get his ice in the summer, but it was not to be on the Dakota prairie. Instead of three years, it took more like twenty years, interspersed with at least four moves, to prove out at farming. In the process, the young pioneer came near bankruptcy, ruined health, and defeat before winning through to success.

Yet in later life, when Almanzo and Laura reminisced about such hard times as they had had, they tended to remember the good old times of schools for singing lessons, weeklong visits with relatives, the gaiety of the little prairie town in Dakota, and their ready ability to make do in each crisis that came to them.

Yes, there were compensations. The Wilders could look back and say that they had finally come to enjoy their ice in both winter and summer.

∾

Everyone is complaining of being tired, of not having time for what they wish to do. . . . It would be a wonderful relief if, by eliminating both wisely and well, life might be simplified.

∾

The object of all education is to make folks fit to live.

∾

It is so easy to be careless and one is so prone to be thoughtless in talking. I told only half of a story the other day, heedlessly overlooking the fact that by telling only a part I left the listeners with a wrong impression of some very kindly person.

The true must come from within.

~

It seems such a pity that we can learn to value what we have only through the loss of it. Truly "we never miss the water till the well runs dry."

~

It is surprising what an opinion one sometimes forms of one's self by mentally standing off and looking on as at a stranger.

~

An untruth is often expressed by silence.

~

How easy and delightful life might be if . . . when we had attained the position we wished, we might rest on our oars and watch the ripples on the stream of life.

~

People in these history-making days hold their opinions so strongly and defend them so fiercely that . . . misunderstandings will come between people who are earnestly striving for the right thing.

Right seems to be obscured and truth is difficult
to find.

～

[People] join in with what they think is popular
opinion until it is almost impossible to tell where
anyone stands on any subject or to do anything
because one cannot tell upon whom to depend.

～

Would you rather have times or things? . . . Things
alone are very unsatisfying. . . . But times would be
bad without some things. We cannot enjoy
ourselves if we are worried over how we shall pay our
bills or the taxes.

～

[A hillbilly] had knocked his enemy down and was
still beating him though he was crying "enough!"
when a stranger came along and interfered.
"Stop! Stop!" the stranger exclaimed. "Don't you
hear him hollering 'enough'?"
"Oh, yes!" replied the hill man, "but he is such a
liar I don't know whether he is telling the truth or
not."

There is a movement in the United States today, widespread and very far-reaching in its consequences. People are seeking after a freer, healthier, happy life.

≈

I thought that everything I read in print was the truth.

≈

Generation after generation, we each must be burned by fire before we will admit that [fire] will burn.

≈

Here on the very peak of the Ozark watershed are to be found good health, good homes, a good living, good times, and good neighbors. What more could anyone want?

≈

Freddie

~

*T*he biggest tragedy Laura's family had to face may not have been Mary's blindness (horrible as that must have been), but the death of Charles Frederick Ingalls, Laura's only brother, in August of 1876 after only nine months of life.

Freddie, as they had come to call him, had never been well, and Ma had often stayed home from church to be as protective of him as possible. But nothing seemed to work to make him stronger, and calling on a doctor in those days was sometimes more dangerous than an illness itself. He was a sickly child who unexpectedly gave a last gasp of life and died on the twenty-seventh of August of that particular year.

Pioneer children died all the time. In the days before vaccination and penicillin, it was commonplace to lose one or more children to unnamed diseases. The Ingalls family would have had plenty of sympathetic support. Still, there it was—the only male child of the family had died.

Freddie's death would have been a terrific blow to Pa. Pa loved his daughters, but he needed a boy to help with the farming. Boys, if they had a will to work, were economic assets back then. There was nothing like today's extended childhood, where the parents don't expect a young man to grow up until he is in his mid-twenties.

Most farmers' sons were considered men by the time they were sixteen. More than likely, what education they had, for good or ill, would have been over by that time, and they would have had an equal share in all the farm labor with the expectation of inheriting the land and whatever progress had been made on it in due time. Since fathers didn't always live to a ripe old age in the late 1800s, the inheritance might come sooner rather than later. Most boys did get something out of the arrangement, though it might seem like unfair child labor to our twentieth-century minds.

From what we do know about Pa Ingalls, he would probably have been a great father to work with, and any son of his would have been a jack-of-all-trades. He would have been a free and independent American, trained to meet all kinds of situations, confident in his abilities, and imbued with the sort of character that brought America to fruition as one of the great democracies of the world in the century that followed.

Pa Ingalls didn't get to see this for his son, but he carried on, took care of his family, and left his moral heritage to his daughters, who made him proud—every one of them. As for his sorrow, of course it ran deep, but you didn't make a big fuss in those days. Even if your dream had just died, you carried on. There wasn't any time to stop and dwell on the big eternal "Why?"

∾

"I don't know what to do with Edith," said a
mother to me. "I've no idea where she learned it,
but she is a regular little liar. I can't depend on a
thing she says."
Just then [Edith] started to go into another room.

"Oh! Don't go in there!" her mother exclaimed.
"It's dark in there and there is a big dog behind the
door." The child opened the door a crack, peeped
around it, smiled a knowing smile, and went on
in. . . .
Where do you suppose Edith learned to be
untruthful?

~

It is easier, for a time, to go with the current; but
how much more can be accomplished if we would all
be honest in our talk. We all despise a coward, but
we sometimes forget there is a moral as well as a
physical cowardice. . . . It is weakness to one's
personality and moral fiber to deny one's opinions
or falsify one's self, while it throws broadcast into
the world just that much more cowardice and
untruth.

~

We would be saved some sorry blunders and many a
heartache if we might begin our knowledge where
our parents leave off . . . but life is not that way.

12
Relationships

"Sweet are the uses of adversity" when it shows us the kindness in our neighbors' hearts.

~

If there is a disagreement between friends and the neighbors begin talking about it, the difficulty grows like a jimson weed, and the more it is talked about the faster it grows.

~

It is not alone "one touch of nature" which "makes the whole world kin," but every emotion which writes itself on the human countenance creates a family likeness with others of its kind, even between people of different races.

~

Our friends and neighbors are either better friends and neighbors today than they were several years ago or they are not so good.

~

"I do like to have you say kinfolks. It seems to mean so much more than relations or relatives," writes my sister from the North. Kinfolks! It is such a homey sounding word and strong, too, and sweet.

[Some] by their bad temper and exacting dispositions estrange their relatives and repel friendly advances. Then they bewail the fact that their friends are so few.

≈

"You have so much tact and can get along with people so well," said a friend to me once. Then, after a thoughtful pause, she added, "But I never could see any difference between tact and trickery."

≈

It is true that we find ourselves reflected in our friends and neighbors, and if we are in the habit of having bad neighbors, we are not likely to find better by changing our location.

≈

If we would not be satisfied until we had passed a share of our happiness on to other people, what a world we could make!

≈

I have known Mrs. Brown for years; and ever since I have known her, she has prided herself on her plain speaking, showing very little regard for others'

feelings. Her unkindness appears . . . but simply an advance in the way she was going years ago. Her dexterity in hurting the feelings of others has grown with practice.

≈

There is something brightening to the wits and cheering to the spirits in congenial crowds that is found in nothing else.

≈

My sympathy is very much with the person who seems to be unable to say the right thing at the proper time. In spite of oneself, there are times when one's mental fingers seem to be all thumbs.

≈

[Shep] once made a mistake and barked savagely at an old friend. . . . Later, as we all sat in the yard, he seemed uneasy. . . . At last he walked deliberately to the visitor, sat up, and held out his paw. It was so plainly an apology that our friend said: "That's all right, Shep, old fellow! Shake and forget it!" Shep shook hands and walked away perfectly satisfied.

Animals

~

*A*ccording to her own account, it was Laura's love of horses, particularly Almanzo's beautifully matched pair of Morgans, that piqued the interest of the girl of sixteen in the young man of twenty-six. Laura loved animals of all kinds, but especially horses.

After she got married, Laura learned how to break or tame her own ponies. She said she didn't want to brag, but they were real "broncos," which meant they were pretty rambunctious. Once, she had to sell one of her horses to pay taxes and it nearly broke her heart.

Still, it was Almanzo who was the horse expert and he had a particular fondness for Morgan horses. Named after Justin Morgan, the horses were noted for their strength, endurance, and speed in spite of their comparatively small size. Almanzo introduced the breed into the Ozarks and had several prizewinners. The fact is, the Wilders took almost as many pictures of their farm animals as they took of themselves.

Mrs. Wilder had a special fondness for dogs, and she had several English bulldogs. Of course, the bulldog named Jack features prominently in many of her books. While living in the Ozarks, she had a bulldog that developed a terrible sore on its jaw. When the animal got to hurting badly, it would come and lay its head in Laura's lap as if to say, "Can you help me?" She would talk to it

and rub some salve on the sore, and eventually the animal got better.

A number of people still living in and around Mansfield, Missouri, remember the Wilder's Airedale, a remarkably intelligent animal named Ring because of a complete dark circle around one eye. This dog was such a part of the family that he ate with them at the table, off a plate.

Mrs. Wilder had cats, too, but people didn't remember her as a cat person. The truth is, she always had too many cats and was always trying to give some of them away.

The Wilders liked to name their animals, and every farm animal had a name, including their goats, of which Almanzo had quite a herd. He had them trained so that they would come to him and stand on a box while he milked them. He had one old male goat the neighborhood boys liked to tease, but they always stayed on the safe side of the fence when they did their pestering.

Mrs. Wilder, who outlived her husband by eight years, always had some sort of pet around. Those last years were lonely and she appreciated the company.

∾

Sometimes we find ourselves in a way so narrow
that it is impossible to meet others on a common

ground without being torn by brambles of
misunderstanding and prejudice.

~

As much good can be done by the right kind of
gossip as harm by the wrong sort. Ever hear of
golden gossip? A woman who was always talking
about her friends and neighbors made it her
business to talk of them, in fact, never said
anything but good of them. She was a gossip, but it
was "golden gossip."

~

I wonder if you all know the story of the man
who was moving from one place to another
because he had such bad neighbors. Just before
making the change, he met a man from the
neighborhood to which he was going and told
him in detail how mean his old neighbors were.
Then he asked the other man what the neighbors
were like in the place to which he was moving.
The other man replied, "You will find just the
same kind of neighbors where you are going as
those you leave behind you."

There was once a small boy with a quarrelsome disposition and a great unwillingness to obey the rules his mother made. At school he would seek a quarrel and get the thrashing he deserved; then he would come home, disobey his mother, and be punished. Then he would sit and wail, "O-o-h! I always get the worst of it! I don't know why, but at school and everywhere I always get the worst of it!"

≈

I read a little verse a few years ago entitled, "If We Only Understood," and the refrain was "We would love each other better,/If we only understood." I have forgotten the author . . . but the refrain comes to my mind every now and then when I hear unkind remarks.

≈

Songs in the Evening

One of the most touching things that Pa did in saying good-bye to Laura when she and Almanzo and their daughter, Rose, left De Smet to settle in the Ozarks was to promise her that she would inherit his fiddle when he passed on. This gesture greatly moved Laura, for although none of the girls had learned to play it, Pa's fiddle and the music it brought into Laura's life were to be immortalized when she wrote about her family thirty-five years later.

Mrs. Wilder's books contain an astonishing number of references to music and the part it played in the family's evening recreation. Pa seldom felt so worn down by a day that he couldn't pick up his violin and give a lift to his spirits by singing "Old Dan Tucker."

> *Get out of the way for old Dan Tucker!*
> *He's too late to get his supper!*
> *Supper's over and the dishes washed,*
> *Nothing left but a piece of squash!*

Or, perhaps the now unfamiliar "Old Tubal Cain."

> *Old Tubal Cain was a man of might,*
> *In the days when the earth was young.*
> *By the fierce red light of his furnace bright,*
> *The strokes of his hammer rung . . .*

The various verses don't make a whole lot of sense, but as Pa might say, the tune did "cheer a body up."

As a writer, Laura didn't just throw in these references to the songs and hymns of her childhood to add a dash of color to the story. Correspondence between her and Rose over the writing of the books indicates that

Laura was a stickler for authenticity. When daughter Rose suggested that the old hymn "Dwelling in Beulah Land" might be included in one story as being a song they would likely have sung, Laura insisted that it be left out because they never sang it. And indeed a check of an old hymnal shows that "Dwelling in Beulah Land" wasn't written until 1911. Old, but not old enough.

As was perhaps befitting for a pioneer household, they sang a lot of songs about being on a pilgrim journey, a sometimes wearying pilgrim journey. "In the Sweet By and By" was a favorite of the Ingallses that expressed the essence of many of these now forgotten songs.

> *There's a land that is fairer than day,*
> *And by faith we can see it afar;*
> *For the Father waits over the way,*
> *To prepare us a dwelling-place there.*

Chorus:
> *In the sweet by and by,*
> *We shall meet on that beautiful shore;*
> *In the sweet by and by,*
> *We shall meet on that beautiful shore.*

For fear of giving offense, many persons agree to
anything that is proposed.

~

Shafts of malice aimed in anger forever fall
harmless against the armor of a smile, kind words,
and gentle manners.